FINS TO WINGS

Design	David West Children's Book Design
Designer	Flick Killerby
Editorial Planning	Clark Robinson Limited
Science Editor	Catherine Warren
Researcher	Emma Krikler
Illustrator	Creative Hands
Consultant	Peter Zammit, physiologist

First published in
the United States in 1992 by
Gloucester Press Inc.
95 Madison Avenue
New York, NY 10016

Library of Congress Cataloging-in-Publication Data

Hemsley, William.
    Fins to wings : projects with biology / by William Hemsley.
      p. cm. -- (Hands on science)
    Includes index.
    Summary: Highlights various methods of locomotion used by
animals, and examines the variety of muscles and nerves needed to
move them. Features projects throughout.
    ISBN 0-531-17271-6
    1. Animal locomotion--Juvenile literature. [1. Animal locomotion.]
I. Title. II. Series.
QP301.H37   1992
591.1'852--dc20   91-34410   CIP   AC

Printed in Belgium

HANDS · ON · SCIENCE

FINS TO WINGS

William Hemsley

GLOUCESTER PRESS
New York · London · Toronto · Sydney

CONTENTS

This book is about the ways in which animals move, in water, on land and in the air. It tells you about the skeletons and muscles that provide the machinery for movement. And it describes and explains the many different techniques that animals use to move, from swimming with fins to flying with wings. There are "hands on" projects for you to try and "did you know?" panels of information for fun.

Science ideas with photographs and diagrams

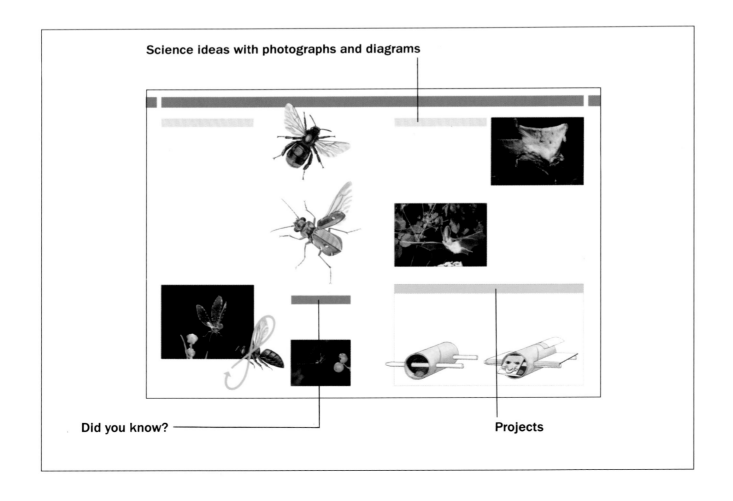

Did you know?

Projects

INTRODUCTION

We can see movement all around us. In the living world (with few exceptions) only animals can move from one place to another using their own energy.

When you look at an animal, many of the things you first see are connected with movement. The animal may have legs, fins or wings. The animal's whole shape may help it to move. For example, a fish may be shaped to move easily through water. If you could see inside an animal, you would see many other structures to do with movement, such as muscles and bones.

There are many reasons why animals move. They search for food and water. They escape from danger and discomfort. They move to find shelter or a mate. In fact, most parts of an animal's life involve some kind of movement.

Animals move in nearly every environment on Earth. They swim in the oceans, walk on land and fly through the air. To do this, animals have developed many, very varied ways of moving.

A bee can move both by flying and walking.

Skeletons have three main functions. First, they support the body of an animal and keep it rigid. Second, they are involved in movement. Third, hard skeletons can provide protection for delicate parts of an animal's body. There are three main types of skeleton: hydrostatic, external and internal.

HYDROSTATIC SKELETONS

Many soft-bodied animals, such as earthworms, have hydrostatic skeletons. A hydrostatic skeleton is like a bag filled with water: the outer layers of the animal's body surround a fluid-filled cavity. Water cannot be compressed (its volume cannot be made less by pressing). This means that if the outer layers of the animal press inward on the fluid, the fluid presses back and supports the animal's body. A hydrostatic skeleton helps with movement because muscles can push on different parts of the fluid, changing the body's shape. But a hydrostatic skeleton does not give the animal any protection.

EXTERNAL SKELETONS

Many animals, such as insects, spiders and crabs, have external skeletons (known as exoskeletons). The skeleton covers the outside of the animal's body. Exoskeletons are made of a strong substance called chitin (pronounced ky-tin). They also contain proteins and calcium carbonate to make them harder. The skeleton is made up of three layers. The middle layer has spaces to make it lighter.

Exoskeletons do not bend easily and so provide support for an animal's body. Muscles for movement are attached to the inside of the skeleton. Exoskeletons give very good protection. But it is difficult for an animal to grow inside an exoskeleton because the skeleton itself cannot grow. The skeleton has to be molted and regrown from time to time as the animal gets bigger.

△ A hydrostatic skeleton supports an earthworm's body, and is also very flexible.

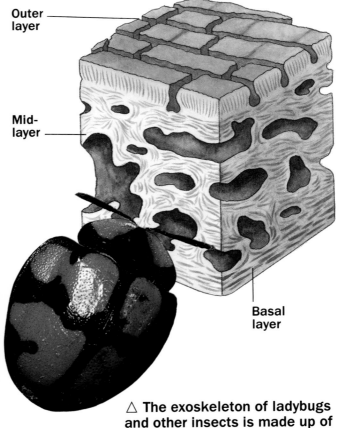

Outer layer

Mid-layer

Basal layer

△ The exoskeleton of ladybugs and other insects is made up of three layers.

INTERNAL SKELETONS

Birds, fish, amphibians, reptiles and mammals all have internal skeletons (known as endoskeletons). Endoskeletons are inside an animal's body and are made of bone and cartilage (except for primitive fish like sharks, which have only cartilage). Bone is very hard and strong, and is made of 70 percent minerals and 30 percent proteins. Cartilage is similar to bone, but is made mostly of proteins and is softer.

Endoskeletons give support and help with movement in much the same way as exoskeletons do. But they provide protection only with special structures — such as the skull to protect the brain. Another advantage of endoskeletons is that they allow an animal to grow more easily — the bone just grows at the same rate as the rest of the animal's body.

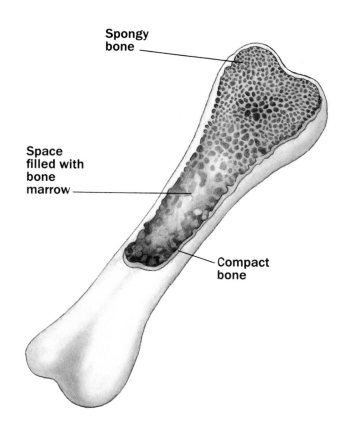

Spongy bone

Space filled with bone marrow

Compact bone

△ A typical bone has three regions. Compact bone is hard. So is spongy bone, but with air spaces. Bone marrow is soft.

▽ A mammal's skeleton (here, a cat's) has very many bones.

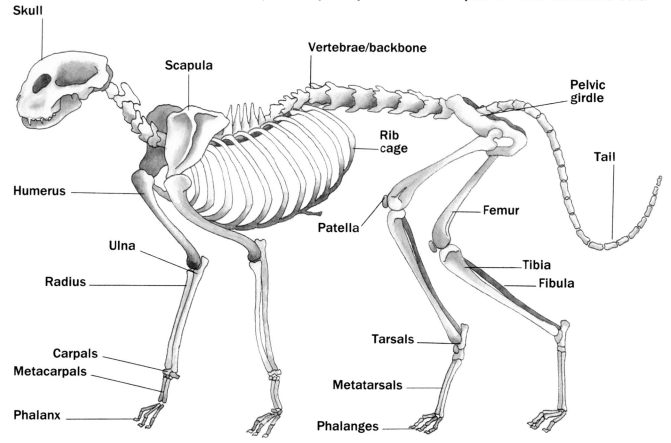

Skull

Scapula

Vertebrae/backbone

Pelvic girdle

Tail

Rib cage

Humerus

Femur

Ulna

Patella

Radius

Tibia

Fibula

Carpals

Metacarpals

Tarsals

Phalanx

Metatarsals

Phalanges

FEET

The bones in the feet of an animal reflect how it moves. A pigeon's feet help it to balance on two legs and to grip on perches. A frog has hind feet it can use in walking, but they are also shaped like flippers for swimming. A gorilla can stand on two legs, and the shape of the bones in its feet is quite like that of a bird. A horse stands on four feet, each with only one toe. Its feet are designed for running quickly, and not for balance.

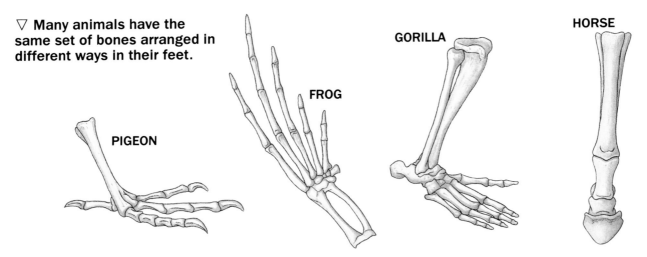

▽ Many animals have the same set of bones arranged in different ways in their feet.

PIGEON

FROG

GORILLA

HORSE

JOINTS

If an animal's skeleton did not have joints, the animal would not be able to move. A joint is where two bones meet. Some joints, known as fixed joints, cannot move (for example, in the skull). Most joints can move, however, and these can be divided into three main types.

Hinge joints are like a hinge on a door: they can bend in only one direction. An example in humans is the knee. Ball-and-socket joints allow movement in many directions. Examples are the hip and shoulder joints. The third type of joint is the pivot (or sliding, or slipping) joint. This consists of two flat ends of bone meeting. The two ends slide over each other, which allows a small amount of bending and rotating. There are examples of pivot joints in the wrists and ankles. (The joints of animals with external skeletons allow similar movements, but are made differently – see page 11.)

In joints, synovial fluid acts like oil for pads of cartilage that protect the bones from wear and tear.

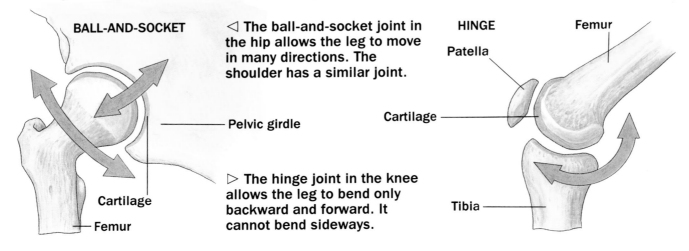

BALL-AND-SOCKET

◁ The ball-and-socket joint in the hip allows the leg to move in many directions. The shoulder has a similar joint.

Pelvic girdle

Cartilage

Femur

▷ The hinge joint in the knee allows the leg to bend only backward and forward. It cannot bend sideways.

HINGE

Femur

Patella

Cartilage

Tibia

LIGAMENTS AND TENDONS

Like cartilage, ligaments and tendons are made mostly of protein. The cartilage in a joint prevents the ends of the bones from being damaged by rubbing against each other. The ligaments hold the ends of the bones together. Ligaments are cords, bands or sheets of tissue that surround a joint. They are strong, but quite elastic to allow the joint to move. Some joints have one sheet of ligament surrounding the whole joint.

Tendons connect muscles to bones. Muscles that bring about movement must be connected to bones because they need something to pull against. The connection is usually close to a joint. Tendons are very strong, but much less elastic than ligaments. It would not help an animal to move if, when a muscle pulled, it merely stretched a tendon.

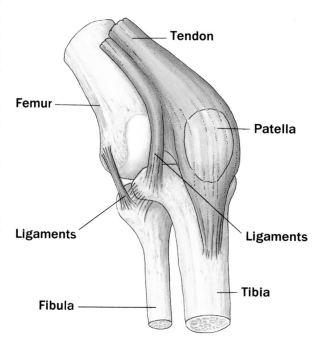

▽ The knee is a complicated joint, surrounded by many ligaments and tendons.

Tendon

Femur

Patella

Ligaments

Ligaments

Tibia

Fibula

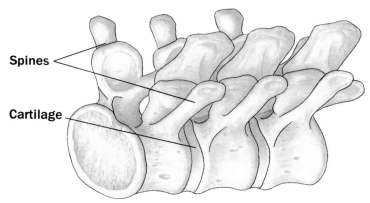

Spines

Cartilage

◁ The bones of the backbone are connected by pivot joints. In four-legged animals, there are spines sticking up from the backbone. These are connected by ligaments. The ligaments are like the girders of a bridge and give the backbone extra strength.

EXPERIMENT

Get an adult to help you cut three corks in half across their middles. Cut a piece of thick cardboard about 4 inches long and 1 inch wide. Glue a piece of cork in place at each end. Put the "bridge" on a flat surface, and press down in the middle. How easily does it bend? Now make the structure shown in the second diagram, using glue. Press down in the middle again. How easily does it bend this time? This structure is like the bones and ligaments in the spine of a four-legged animal.

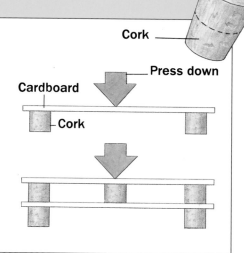

Cork

Press down

Cardboard

Cork

Muscles produce movement in animals. Most animals have large numbers of muscles. Muscles carry out work by contracting (getting shorter). There is more than one type of muscle — for example, in mammals, heart muscle is a special type. The muscles that produce movement are known as skeletal muscles.

STRUCTURE

Muscles are made mostly of three types of protein. These proteins together make up muscle fibrils. If you look at a fibril using a microscope, you can see light and dark bands. Each band is made largely of one type of protein. When the fibril contracts, chemical actions pull these bands of protein together so that they overlap. The fibril becomes shorter. This process uses up energy.

The fibrils are bundled together to make muscle fibers. Each fiber is in many ways like a cell, but has more than one nucleus. The fibers are bundled together to make larger bundles, which in turn make up the complete muscle. Each bundle is surrounded by a membrane (a thin sheet of connective tissue). At each end of a muscle, the membranes (particularly the outermost one) and the fibers connect to a tendon (page 9).

Muscle contractions are controlled by nerves. When a nerve message reaches a muscle fiber, the end of the nerve releases chemicals that cause the fiber to contract. Muscle fibers have what is called an "all-or-nothing response." This means that a fiber either contracts completely or does not contract at all. Differences in the distance a muscle contracts and the strength with which it contracts result from differences in the numbers of fibers contracting.

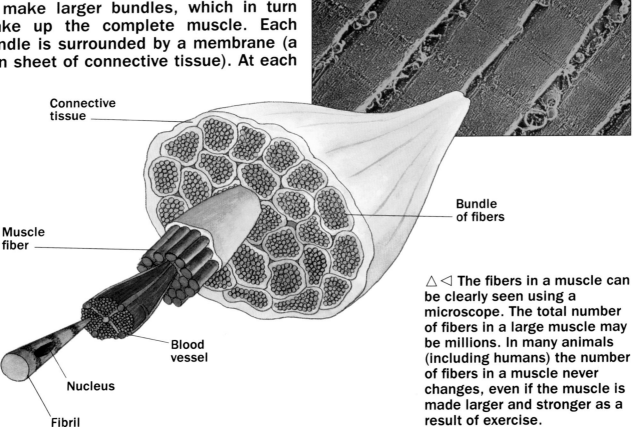

Connective tissue

Bundle of fibers

Muscle fiber

Blood vessel

Nucleus

Fibril

△ ◁ The fibers in a muscle can be clearly seen using a microscope. The total number of fibers in a large muscle may be millions. In many animals (including humans) the number of fibers in a muscle never changes, even if the muscle is made larger and stronger as a result of exercise.

HYDROSTATIC SKELETON

Muscle along the body

Circular muscle

Body cavity

△ With hydrostatic skeletons, the main muscles are arranged straight along the body and in rings around the body.

EXTERNAL SKELETON

Muscle

Flexible chitin

△ In the joints of external skeletons, two parts of the skeleton are connected by flexible chitin. The joint is moved by pairs of muscles.

▷ There are about 60 muscles in the human leg (only the main ones are shown). When the leg is bent and supporting weight, the muscles in the calf, the front of the thigh and the buttocks are working. When the leg is straight, most of the muscles are relaxed.

FUNCTION

The movement of skeletal muscles is controlled by the brain (except for certain "reflex actions"). Because muscles can only contract and relax, but not expand, they are usually arranged in pairs. Each one of a pair has an opposite effect. For example, the muscles at the front of the human thigh straighten the leg; the muscles at the back bend it. The bones that a muscle is attached to are like levers; a short contraction of a thigh muscle moves the foot a long way.

Muscles in animals with external skeletons work in much the same way as those in animals with internal skeletons. The muscles are still arranged in pairs with opposing effects.

In animals with hydrostatic skeletons, there is nothing solid for muscles to pull against. The muscles therefore pull against each other and against the pressure of fluid in the body.

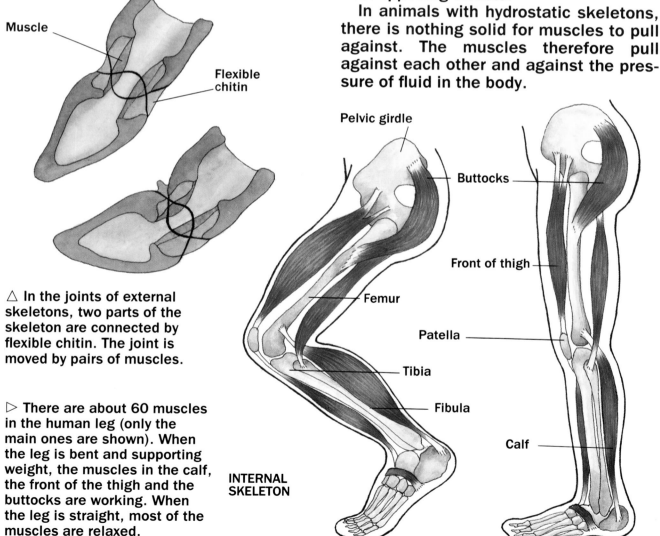

Pelvic girdle

Buttocks

Front of thigh

Femur

Patella

Tibia

Fibula

Calf

INTERNAL SKELETON

The first life on Earth appeared in water. Many animals, including most single-celled and simple animals, still live in water. Single-celled animals do not have any sort of skeleton, or even any real muscles. There are three main methods by which they move: by amoeboid movement, with cilia or with flagella.

AMOEBOID MOVEMENT

A very simple form of movement is found in amoebas (which are tiny single-celled animals). Amoeboid movement relies on the fact that cytoplasm (the jellylike content of the cell) can flow into a tight space in the cell wall to form a projection which extends from the rest of the cell. An amoeba forms pseudopodia (which means "false feet") with its cytoplasm, and then draws the cytoplasm back and forms another pseudopodia in a different place along the cell wall.

An amoeba moves by moving its pseudopodia. Although amoeba live in water, most of their movement occurs when their pseudopodia are in contact with a solid object.

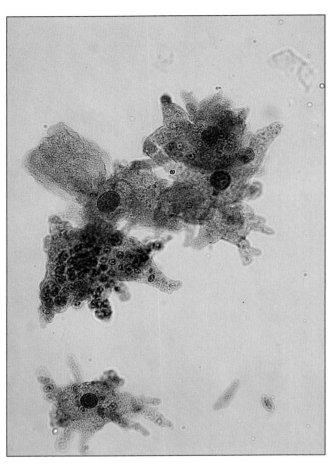

△ Through a microscope, it is possible to see several pseudopodia on all of this group of amoebas.

CILIA

Cilia are used for movement by many single-celled animals and larvae that live in water. Cilia are hairlike structures on the surface of a cell. Each contains filaments (thin strands) that contract to make it move. A basal granule controls a cilium's movement.

Cilia move an animal forward by pushing back against the water. To do this, the cilia become stiff and swing backward (the power stroke). After the power stroke, the cilia move forward again (the recovery stroke). During this stroke, the cilia are relaxed and so do not push against the water. Large numbers of cilia are arranged in patterns and work in a coordinated rhythm.

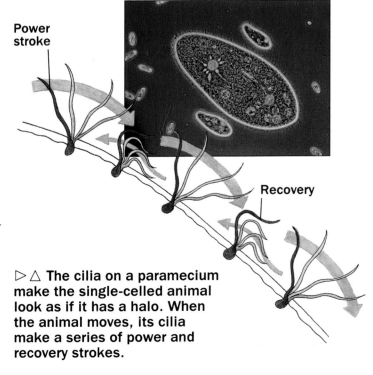

Power stroke

Recovery

▷△ The cilia on a paramecium make the single-celled animal look as if it has a halo. When the animal moves, its cilia make a series of power and recovery strokes.

FLAGELLA

A flagellum is a long thread emerging from a cell. Flagella are like very long cilia. Their structure is similar, but most cells have only one or two flagella. Euglena is an example of an animal that uses a flagellum to move.

A flagellum can produce movement in much the same way as a cilium, by pushing backward against water like an oar. The movement of flagella is, however, often much more complex than this. A flagellum may move in waves (like an eel swimming), pushing the animal along. It may also have a corkscrewlike movement, which has an effect rather like that of a propeller.

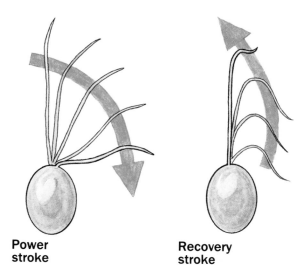

Power stroke

Recovery stroke

△ The basic movements of a flagellum include a power stroke and a recovery stroke, but are often more complex.

△ Scallops swim with an uneven movement.

JET PROPULSION

Some animals swim by shooting out jets of water. Squids, octopuses and cuttlefish do this by drawing water inside their bodies through a tube called a siphon. They then squirt the water out of the siphon, which pushes them along. They can point the siphon to control the direction in which they move.

Scallops, and some other two-shelled shellfish, move by clapping their shells together. When the shells open, water is drawn in. When the shells clap shut, the water shoots out again and the scallop moves along.

JELLYFISH

Jellyfish are not complex animals, although they may be quite large. They do not have skeletons, only a layer of rubbery material called mesoglea. Jellyfish are shaped like an upside down bowl or plate. They move by pulling the edges of this plate together. This movement pushes water down beneath the jellyfish, and so pushes the jellyfish upward. To move along, jellyfish swim at an angle, and so move diagonally upward. They then sink again a bit further along before pushing once more. This gives them a characteristic way of moving.

△ Jellyfish swim very slowly.

BUOYANCY

Buoyancy is the ability of a thing to float. The flesh and bone that an animal is made of are more dense than water, and so it is not buoyant. This means that, unless it has some way of floating, a fish has to keep swimming to stop it from sinking. Swimming all the time uses a lot of energy. Many fish have a swim bladder to stop them from sinking.

A swim bladder is sausage-shaped and filled with air. In some fish, the amount of air in the bladder is controlled by releasing and absorbing air from the blood. In other fish, the swim bladder opens into the throat. The amount of air in the bladder is controlled by taking in or letting out air through the fish's mouth.

Some other animals that live in water have different ways of floating. Cuttlefish, for example, have air-filled spaces in their cuttlebone.

EXPERIMENT

To see how a swim bladder helps a fish to float, you will need a glass bottle (or jar) with a screw top. With the bottle empty, screw on the top and place it in a sink full of water. Then fill the bottle one-quarter full of water and put it in the sink again. Now try with the bottle half, three-quarters and completely full. Then see if you can make the bottle float, but beneath the water's surface.

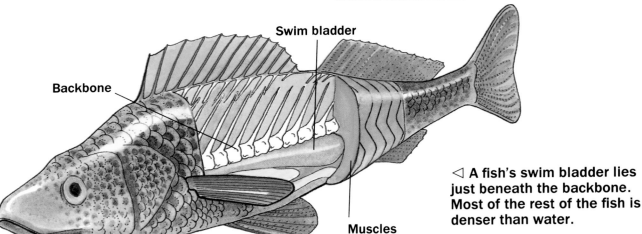

Swim bladder

Backbone

Muscles

◁ A fish's swim bladder lies just beneath the backbone. Most of the rest of the fish is denser than water.

◁ Sharks and their relations do not have swim bladders. If a shark stops swimming, it sinks. A shark's fins are like small wings that keep it up in the water as it moves along. A few sharks that live in deep sea store a light, waxy substance called squalene in their livers, which helps them to float.

STREAMLINING

An object with a shape that lets water (or air) pass over it easily is streamlined. Streamlining is very important for fish. If they could not move through water easily they would waste a lot of energy and travel much more slowly. In order to be streamlined, most fish have a smooth, curved shape. They are often narrow in one direction, for example, across their bodies. Fins and other parts that stick out slope backward.

As well as having a streamlined shape, fish have skin that allows water to pass over it easily. Scales overlap and point backward rather than forward. And fishes' skin is often covered with slippery mucus, which again helps water to pass over it.

△ Most fish, such as the stickleback, are shaped to let water slide over them easily.

▽ Most fish are well streamlined, but the trunk fish has poor streamlining.

STINGRAY   ANGEL FISH   LOACH   TRUNK FISH

EXPERIMENT

You can find out which shapes are best streamlined. Cut three pieces of cardboard, about 6 by 12 inches. Make them into the shapes shown below. Use paper clips where needed. Move the shapes through water in the directions shown by the arrows. Which shape moves most easily? Which is most like a fish?

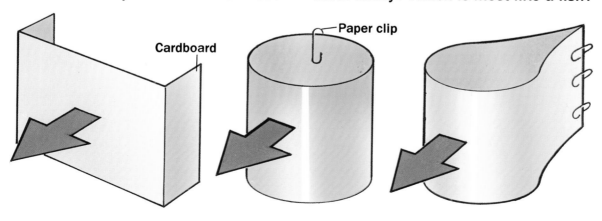

Cardboard

Paper clip

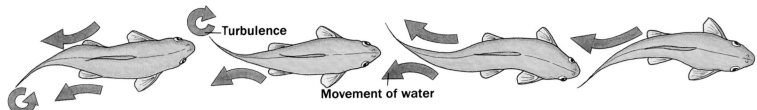

Turbulence

Movement of water

CONTROL AND MOVEMENT

Fish are not only efficient swimmers, but are also very good at controlling their movement in the water. To control movement and to keep themselves stable, fish use their fins.

There are three main ways that a fish can turn in the water. It can "pitch," which is turning up or down; it can "yaw," which is turning to the left or right; and it can "roll," which is turning over sideways.

Different fins are used to control each type of movement. The main functions of the dorsal and anal fins are to control rolling and yawing. The pectoral and pelvic fins are in pairs, with one at each side of the body. Their main function is to control pitch, although in most fish they also help to control rolling and yawing. In fact, the exact functions of each fin vary from one type of fish to another.

The tail fin is also involved in control, but its chief function is in helping with swimming forward. The main method of swimming that most fish use is undulating (waving) their bodies. As a fish undulates its body, water is pushed backward beside the fish, and the fish is pushed forward. The tail helps to increase the effect of the undulations. Some fish move mostly by waving the back ends of their bodies and their tails.

DID YOU KNOW?

Some fish use their fins as legs. Mudskippers live on mudflats and in mangrove swamps in Africa and Asia. When the tide goes out, they use their specially adapted pectoral fins to walk over the mud. Their tails drag along behind them.

▽ The fins on a fish control movement in all directions and keep the fish stable.

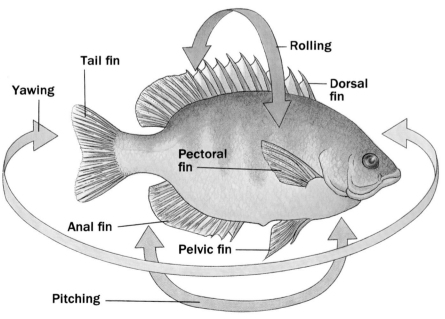

Rolling

Tail fin

Dorsal fin

Yawing

Pectoral fin

Anal fin

Pelvic fin

Pitching

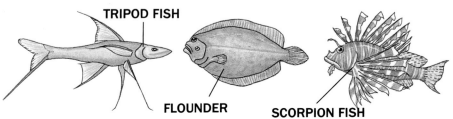

TRIPOD FISH

FLOUNDER

SCORPION FISH

◁ Different fish have very different fins, but all fish use their fins to control movement — even if they use them for other purposes as well, such as camouflage.

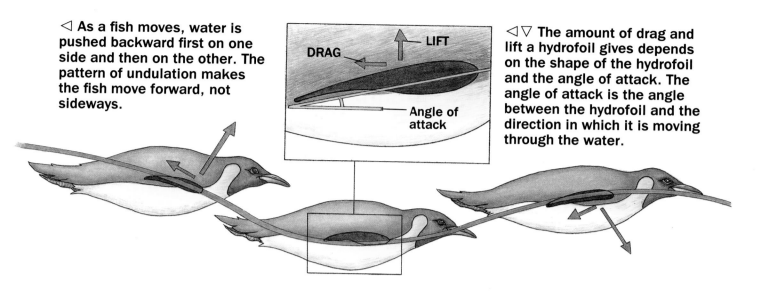

◁ As a fish moves, water is pushed backward first on one side and then on the other. The pattern of undulation makes the fish move forward, not sideways.

LIFT

DRAG

Angle of attack

◁▽ The amount of drag and lift a hydrofoil gives depends on the shape of the hydrofoil and the angle of attack. The angle of attack is the angle between the hydrofoil and the direction in which it is moving through the water.

HYDROFOILS

Another way that animals move forward in water is with hydrofoils. A hydrofoil is like a fin, but stronger and moves the animal along in a special way.

An example of an animal that uses hydrofoils to swim is the penguin. As it moves through the water, it flaps its wings up and down (penguins cannot use their wings to fly). The wing works as the hydrofoil. As the wing moves, water passes over it. This causes forces to act on the wing in rather the same way as they do on an aircraft's wing. A small amount of drag slows the penguin down. But the biggest force is lift. Because of the angle at which the wing moves, part of the lift force is forward (the other part is either upward or downward). The combined effects of the overall shape of the penguin, the drag and the forward part of the lift move the penguin forward. A part of the lift is left over, so the penguin tends to move up and down in the water as it swims.

Other examples of animals that swim with hydrofoils include some fast-moving fish (such as tuna and marlins), which use their tails. Whales and dolphins also use their tails as hydrofoils.

OAR PROPULSION

Another way that animals move through water is with an oar action. Many fish swim in this way when they are moving slowly or maneuvering carefully. They use their fins (especially the pectoral fins) as the oars.

The fins move backward, pushing against the water. This movement forces the fish's body forward. The fish then turns its fins sideways so that they can be moved forward without pushing against the water. When in the forward position, the fins are turned once more and are ready to push again.

△ The water beetle uses one pair of long legs as oars when it is swimming.

Animals that live in water are supported by their buoyancy. Animals that live on land do not have this support and so they feel the full force of gravity. This means that land animals need stronger skeletons. If land animals have legs, the legs must be able to support their weight and have strong muscles.

CRAWLING

Many animals crawl on land without using legs. These animals include snakes, slugs and snails, and worms.

Snakes use two methods of crawling. The first method is curving their bodies into S-shaped curves. The back and front parts of each "S" press against the ground while the middle part moves forward. Series of curves pass along the snake's body. The second method is "walking" with the scales on their bellies and ribs. Some scales press against the ground while others move forward.

Slugs and snails move by sliding on a slippery mucus. The mucus becomes firm when it is pressed, so the animal can move by sending waves of muscle contractions along its belly.

Worms have hydrostatic skeletons, so can lengthen and shorten sections of their bodies. Some parts of a worm's body press against the ground while others become narrower and move forward. The parts that have moved then press on the ground, and other parts move. Most worms move in this way.

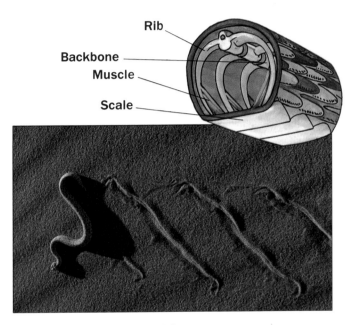

△ Sidewinders move sideways. The head goes forward then the body curves along behind, leaving strange tracks.

WALK

CANTER

DID YOU KNOW?

Millipedes and centipedes have large numbers of legs. Millipedes generally have more than centipedes — the species with the most legs has more than 700! The movement of all the legs is very carefully coordinated so that they do not get muddled up.

PROJECT

Try to observe the different ways that an animal (such as a cat, a dog or a horse) uses its legs when moving at different speeds. Watch especially for the order that it puts its feet down, how it bends its legs, whether the animal moves evenly or up and down, and whether its backbone curves.

▽ Some gaits of a horse, from slowest to fastest, are the walk, trot, canter and gallop.

ON FOUR LEGS

Most mammals have four legs, as do reptiles (except snakes and a few others) and amphibians. There are several advantages to having four legs. It is the smallest even number of legs on which it is easy to balance. An animal can use the whole length of its body to run with by bending its spine (this is very noticeable in the cat family). The weight of the animal is quite evenly supported.

There are many ways of moving four legs. The different ways are known as gaits, and the main difference is in the order in which the feet are put down. Most mammals use more than one gait.

A horse, for example, uses four main gaits, although it can use others. When walking, it lifts its feet in turn and puts them down in the same order. When trotting, it lifts feet at opposite corners, puts them down, then lifts its other two feet. When cantering, one back foot hits the ground, then the other back foot and the front foot on the opposite side together, then the other front foot. When galloping, all four legs hit the ground singly, first the hind then the front legs.

TROT

GALLOP

ON TWO FEET

There is one big advantage in having two feet for animals with four limbs. It means that only two limbs are used for walking, so the other two limbs can be used for something else. Birds use their other pair of limbs as wings. Humans have two legs because their other limbs have hands. Human hands are highly skilled and too delicate to be used for walking.

There are disadvantages in having only two legs. It is generally more difficult to run quickly. Another problem is that all of the animal's weight is on just two legs. But the biggest problem is balance.

Most birds cannot walk, run or hop very well (although some birds that do not fly can run very quickly). Most birds move using their wings, however, so walking well is not very important. It is more important for flying that their legs are light. Birds' feet stick out quite a long way from their legs to help balance.

Human feet also stick out from the legs, but are more complex than birds'

feet. They have muscles of their own and take an active part in both balance and walking. Humans have only two normal gaits: walking and running. In both, the feet move in turn — first one moves forward, then the other. In walking, at least one foot is in contact with the ground at all times. In running, neither foot touches the ground between strides.

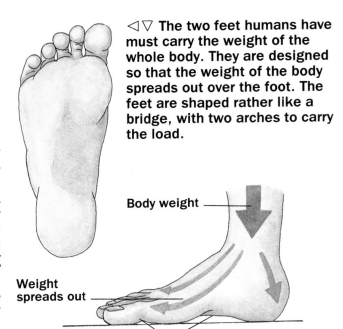

◁▽ The two feet humans have must carry the weight of the whole body. They are designed so that the weight of the body spreads out over the foot. The feet are shaped rather like a bridge, with two arches to carry the load.

Body weight

Weight spreads out

Arches

ENERGY

The energy in the body of a walking human is provided by the muscles in the legs. If human legs were perfectly frictionless wheels, one push would keep a person going for a long time. However, as people walk, their legs hit the ground, which loses energy.

The type of energy in a walking person changes during each step. When one leg is straight and vertical, the body has a lot of potential energy. This is because the body is at its highest from the ground. This is like a pendulum at the top of its swing, which has potential energy that will make it swing downward. When one leg is pushing and the other is stretched out in front, the body has more kinetic energy (energy of movement). This is like a pendulum at the bottom of its swing when it is moving fast. Similar changes in energy occur when a person runs.

▽ The amounts of potential and kinetic energy in the body change with each step.

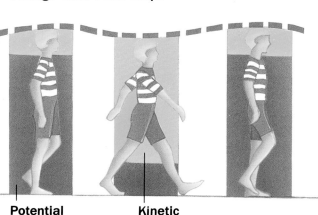

Potential energy

Kinetic energy

PROJECT

Humans have two normal gaits (walking and running), but how many other ways can you think of for moving along the ground? Try them for yourself. Are some very difficult? Do you find that most ways use a lot of energy for traveling a short distance?

HOPPING

Hopping is moving along by jumping with two legs, and with both legs moving at the same time. Some hopping animals, such as frogs, can also walk on four legs — if not very well. But their main method of moving is by hopping.

Animals that hop need one pair of large, powerful legs — almost always the back legs. The hopping legs must be strong because they provide all the energy for movement. They must be large to carry large muscles, and also to provide long levers to push the animal forward.

Animals hop in different ways and for different reasons. Frogs have long back legs for swimming, which are almost "ready-made" for hopping. Frogs hop in single bounds, stopping between each hop. Frogs land on their short front legs.

Fleas hop to land on an animal from which they will suck blood. They cannot fly, so hopping is the best way to move quickly from one animal to another or from the ground onto an animal.

Kangaroos are very good hoppers. When they are moving fast, they can keep up a steady movement — without stopping between hops in the way that a frog does. Kangaroos use their short front legs to lean on when they are bending down to feed from the ground.

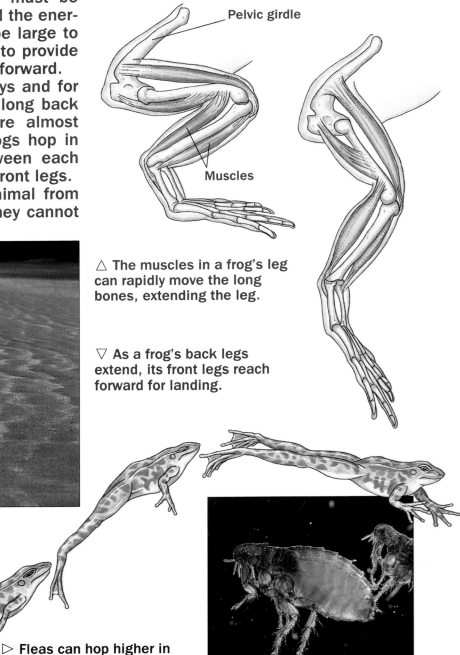

Pelvic girdle

Muscles

△ The muscles in a frog's leg can rapidly move the long bones, extending the leg.

▽ As a frog's back legs extend, its front legs reach forward for landing.

△ A kangaroo's long, heavy tail helps it to balance as it hops along in large bounds.

▷ Fleas can hop higher in relation to their size than any other animal.

DID YOU KNOW?

Ducks waddle as they walk. The reason is that their legs are arranged for paddling through water more than for walking. To paddle well, the legs are attached far apart on the body. This means that when a duck lifts one leg, it tends to fall over toward that side. To avoid this, ducks rock from side to side as they walk.

▷ A gorilla's foot closely resembles a human foot. Gorillas spend most of their time on the ground and often walk on two feet. A gibbon's foot has a very long "big toe." Gibbons spend most of their time in trees, and this long toe helps them to grip branches. A gibbon's hand has a short thumb. This is because they use the hand like a hook for swinging on branches, and a long thumb would get in the way. Gibbons often use their feet rather than their hands to hold small objects.

GORILLA'S FOOT

GIBBON'S FOOT

GIBBON'S HAND

Very long arm bones

Long bones in hands

▷ The skeleton of a gibbon in many ways resembles a human skeleton, but the bones of the limbs are much longer to help it swing through the trees.

ON TWO HANDS!

Many monkeys and apes use their hands for moving. Also, their feet often resemble hands more than feet. The reason is that these animals spend a lot of their lives in trees. Their limbs are designed for gripping onto branches and moving through the branches.

Perhaps the most specialized tree-living ape is the gibbon. Gibbons move rapidly through the trees, swinging from branch to branch. A gibbon's hands are specially adapted for gripping quickly and firmly onto branches. Gibbons have long arms and legs to reach between branches and to give them a long swing. Their bones are quite thin to make their bodies lighter. This gives the hands less weight to support.

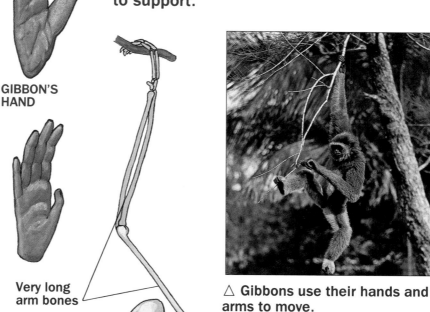

△ Gibbons use their hands and arms to move.

Long bones in legs and feet

Bones are thin to make skeleton light

Animals that fly have many special characteristics. The most obvious of these is wings, but there are other specializations. Flying animals often have light skeletons and a streamlined shape. Animals that use powered flight have very large and powerful muscles to move their wings.

WINGS

There are two main types of wing. The wings of bats and insects are made of skin or thin membranes (as are the flaps on gliding animals). Birds have wings made from feathers.

The bones of a bird's wing are basically the same bones as in the front limbs of other animals with a bony skeleton — although specially adapted. There are several types of feather, but a flight feather is made up firstly of a stem. The stem is rigid; one part (the quill) is embedded in the skin around the wing bones; the other part (the rachis) has barbs attached on two sides. The barbs are long, thin and flexible. They are linked together by barbules.

△ A bird in flight.

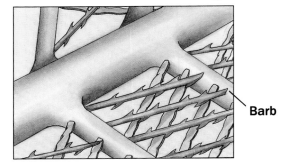

▽ The barbs of a bird's feather are linked with barbules. Some barbules have hooks and some are smooth. Powerful muscles attached to the large breast-bone move the wing.

Barb

▷ The bones and feathers of a bird's wing form a complex structure.

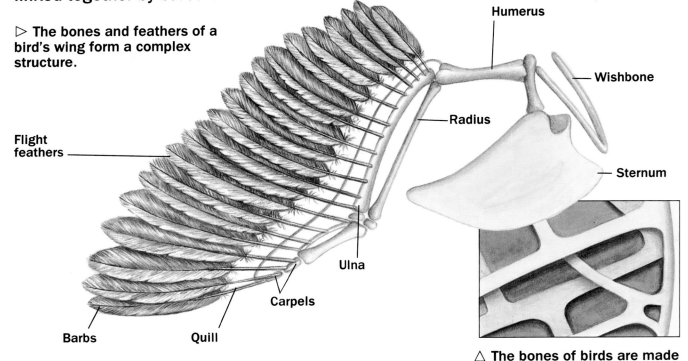

Humerus

Wishbone

Radius

Sternum

Flight feathers

Ulna

Carpels

Barbs

Quill

△ The bones of birds are made lighter by air spaces.

BIRD FLIGHT

There are three main types of flight: gliding, soaring and powered flight. Birds use all three types.

In gliding flight, a bird holds its wings out without moving them. The wings work in the same way as the wings of an aircraft. Because of the wings' shape, air passes more quickly over the top of the wings than underneath. This means that air pressure on top of the wings is less than underneath. The result is an upward force (called lift) on the wings. The bird keeps moving forward because it is dropping under the force of gravity. So the power for the flight comes from the bird's

△ Large birds can soar for long periods of time.

own weight. The problem with gliding is that the bird must start high up and will eventually reach the ground.

In soaring flight, a bird's wings work in the same way as in gliding flight. However, the bird places itself in rising currents of air. The rising air lifts the bird, so that it gains height rather than losing it. The rising currents are often known as thermals. Thermals are columns of warm air that have been heated by areas of hot ground. Rising currents of air also occur where wind hits sharply rising ground, such as a cliff. It is mostly large birds with big wings that soar.

Powered flight involves a bird flapping its wings. As the wings flap downward, the feathers close up and overlap. This gives the greatest resistance to the air. The movement of the wings pushes against the air. The way in which the wings move and their shape give a combination of lift and forward thrust. When the wings flap up again, they rotate and bend, and the feathers open up. This gives the least resistance to air so that the bird is not pushed downward again.

△ Hummingbirds can hover to sip nectar from flowers.

INSECT FLIGHT

Insects' wings consist of thin, quite stiff membranes. Insects with wings have either one or two pairs of wings (although many insects have no wings at all). Various insects use their wings in rather different ways. The main difference, however, is between insects that have two pairs of wings. Some — such as dragonflies — move their pairs of wings alternately: as one pair moves up, the other moves down. Others — such as bees — move all four wings together.

Most insects use only powered flight. They are too light for controlled gliding and soaring. An insect's wings work in much the same way as a bird's wings. As the wings flap down, they push against the air, creating lift and forward movement. However, on the upward stroke, there are no feathers that can let air through. As a result, an insect has to turn its wings quite hard to avoid being pushed down. Butterflies, which cannot turn their wings far, fly with a very jagged movement. Most insects move their wings very fast, which creates a buzzing noise as they fly.

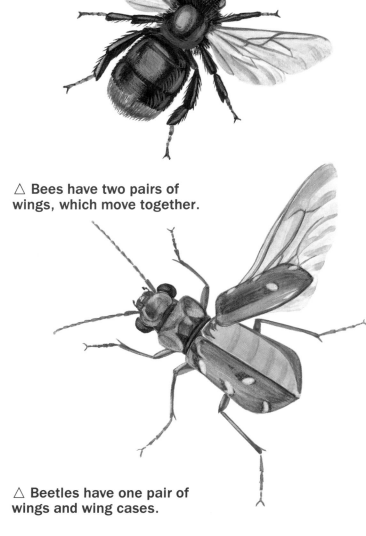

△ Bees have two pairs of wings, which move together.

△ Beetles have one pair of wings and wing cases.

DID YOU KNOW?

Some very light spiders can drift using their silk. They let out the thread until it becomes caught in the wind.

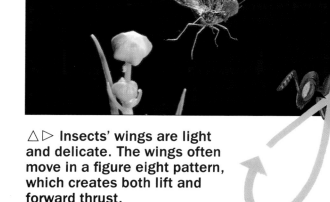

△▷ Insects' wings are light and delicate. The wings often move in a figure eight pattern, which creates both lift and forward thrust.

MAMMALS AND OTHERS

Bats are the only mammals that can use powered flight. They have wings made of skin. The skin is supported by very long, bony fingers. Their wing movements are like those of birds, but they do not have feathers that can let air through. As in birds, bats have powerful flying muscles attached to a large breastbone. Bats fly at night. They find their way by letting out high-pitched squeaks and listening to the echoes. This is why they have large ears and strangely-shaped snouts.

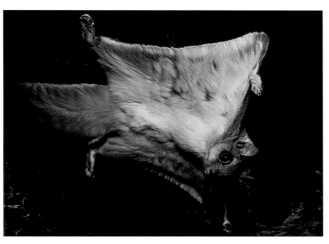

△ A flying squirrel has large flaps of skin and a flat tail.

△ Bats are skillful fliers and hunt for insects at night.

A large number of other animals can glide, but do not have real wings and cannot soar or use powered flight. Flying squirrels have large flaps of skin between their front and back legs. They glide from high up in trees. Flying frogs have large webbed feet that they use to glide — they too glide from trees. Flying snakes and lizards also have flaps of skin along the sides of their bodies. Flying fish have large fins that they can spread out to use as wings. They swim quickly, then shoot out of the water to glide for short distances through the air.

EXPERIMENT

You can find out how flying squirrels jump farther from trees by gliding. Push two empty ballpoint pens or blunt pencils through a cardboard tube from the middle of a toilet paper roll, as shown in the picture. Put a lump of modeling clay in the front. Carefully throw the tube front-first from the top of a flight of stairs — make sure that nobody is at the bottom. Now, using tape and thin cardboard, add flaps between the legs, a wide tail and a head. Try throwing the "squirrel" again.

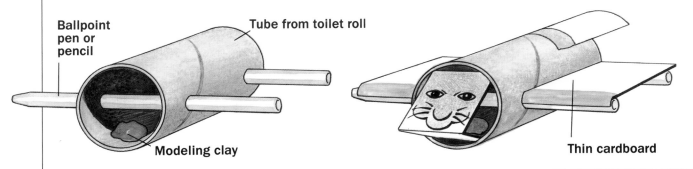

Ballpoint pen or pencil

Tube from toilet roll

Modeling clay

Thin cardboard

Behavior is the way in which animals act and the way they respond to things that are around them. The main way that animals show their behavior is by moving. This may be the kind of movement that has been discussed in the book. But there are other kinds of movement, such as the expressions on a human face.

REASONS FOR MOVING

Animals move for many different reasons. For example, an animal might be searching for food, running away from danger, or finding a place to rest. Sometimes the movement is a direct response to a stimulus (something that affects an animal). Examples of this are when an animal smells food and walks toward it, or when an antelope sees a lion and runs away. Many other parts of an animal's behavior are much more complex, with no obvious direct stimulus. For example, some species of bird gather in flocks and migrate at certain times of year. Another example might be animals fighting for territory.

It is extremely difficult to explain complex behavior. There is a great deal that biologists do not understand. However, the study of behavior is an important part of modern biology.

CONTROL OF MOVEMENT

Muscles are controlled by nerves. These nerves are called motor nerves or motor neurons. All nerves carry messages in the form of electrical signals, which are carried by chemical actions in nerves. A motor nerve is attached to a muscle by what are called motor endplates. When a nerve message reaches motor end plates, the plates release special chemical substances. These substances stimulate the muscle fibers to contract. A large number of motor nerves control the contraction of each muscle.

△ In herds, all of the animals may behave in the same way, such as in a stampede.

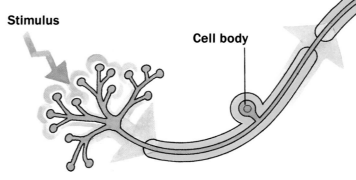

Stimulus

Cell body

△ A sudden stimulus may cause an animal to jump.

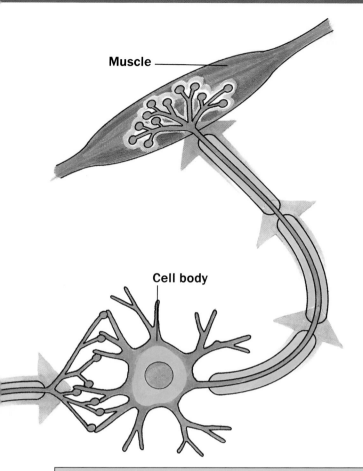

Muscle

Cell body

◁ The system of a sensory nerve connected to a motor nerve, which is in turn connected to a muscle, is known as a reflex arc. It permits very quick reactions to sudden stimuli.

In simple "reflex actions," the signal in a motor nerve comes from a sensory nerve by way of the spinal cord. For example, a sensory nerve in a hand may be stimulated by intense heat. A signal passes to the motor nerve, which causes the hand to pull away from the heat.

The actions of muscles are more often controlled by the brain. Nerve messages are sent to the muscles from the brain by way of motor nerves. For example, when an animal sees food, the brain may give instructions to the muscles to move toward the food, pick it up and eat it. Even this quite simple behavior needs many complex instructions.

PROJECT

You can watch the behavior of animals. Look out first of all for simple behavior — such as hunting for food. You can also look for more complex behavior. Examples might be when two animals meet. A cat may raise its tail and arch its back to threaten another cat. A dog may hold back its ears in submission if threatened by a larger dog. Another example to look for is courtship behavior when an animal is trying to find a mate. Take notes of the behavior that you see. You can draw diagrams of how the animals behave. Think about what you see in terms of muscles being controlled by nerves and by the brain.

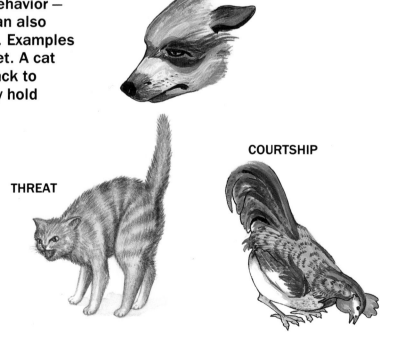

SUBMISSION

THREAT

COURTSHIP

It is difficult to measure such things as the fastest speeds at which animals can run. Animals will not run as fast as possible over a measured distance in a straight line! Scientists, however, do have a reasonably good idea of many movement records for animals.

The fastest land animal is the cheetah. Estimates of its speed over short distances are as high as 60 miles per hour (m/h). A cheetah cannot keep up a high speed for more than about 1,700 feet. The fastest animals in water are the tuna and the cosmopolitan sailfish. Both have been estimated as moving at just over 60 m/h. In the air, the fastest movers are falcons. These birds sometimes dive from great heights and may then travel at over 150 m/h.

Some animals move very slowly. The slowest mammal is the three-toed sloth. It lives in trees and its fastest speed is about 0.15 m/h.

There are many other movement records. For example, the deepest diving

△ Sperm whales are the deepest-diving mammals.

△ The three-toed sloth is the slowest-moving mammal.

fish known is the *Bassogigas*, which has been found at depths of more than 26,500 feet. The deepest diving mammal is the sperm whale, which can reach a depth of about 3,400 feet. Birds, on the other hand, can reach great heights. Vultures have been known to fly at over 33,000 feet. The largest wingspan belongs to the wandering albatross: usually about 2 feet.

△ The cheetah is the fastest-moving animal on land.

△ The wandering albatross has the largest wingspan.

backbone
The row of connected bones that runs along the back of many animals. A thick tube of nerves (the spinal cord) runs through the center of the bones.

buoyancy
The ability of a thing to float. Buoyancy depends on the density (the weight of a certain volume) of the object or material. For example, lead is less buoyant than wood.

cell
The basic unit from which living tissue is made. In animals, cells are separated from other cells by a thin membrane, and most cells have a nucleus.

drag
The resistance to a solid object moving through a gas (such as air) or a liquid (such as water).

force
An influence that makes an object move or change direction. For example, air pressure on a wing is a force.

gait
The way in which an animal uses its legs to move.

lift
An upward force — in animals, usually on a wing or a fin.

limb
A leg, arm, wing, fin, or similar structure on an animal.

mammal
An animal that has a backbone, warm blood, gives birth to live young, and feeds its young on milk. Humans, cats, mice and whales are all mammals.

membrane
A thin, flexible sheet of material. There are many different membranes in animals, including those surrounding cells, around muscle fibers and in the wings of insects.

nucleus
The part of a cell that contains the information necessary for the cell to function and reproduce itself.

organism
Any living thing — such as an animal.

reflex action
An action that is directly in response to a stimulus, without the brain being involved. For example, blinking at a sudden bright light.

stimulus
Anything that affects the movement, behavior, or control systems (such as the nerves) of a living organism.

streamlined
Having a shape that moves easily through a gas or a liquid, without causing large amounts of turbulence.

tissue
A group of cells or a material of a particular type in an organism. For example, muscle fibers are one type of tissue; bone is another type.

tracks
The marks that an animals leaves behind as it moves (such as footprints).

turbulence
Swirling movement in a gas or a liquid. Turbulence is caused when an object moves through a gas or liquid. The more streamlined an object is, the less turbulence it causes.

Photographic Credits:
All the pictures in this book have been supplied by Bruce Coleman Limited apart from: pages 20-21 all: Roger Vlitos; page 27 top: Richard Alan Wood/Animals Animals/OSF; page 28 bottom: Planet Earth Pictures.

PRINTED IN BELGIUM BY

INTERNATIONAL BOOK PRODUCTION